JOB'S JEOPARDY

Do you feel you are like Job?

Then do what Job did—he got himself out of his miserable situation by gaining correct knowledge of the ways and purposes of God.

Secondly, he humbled himself and repented of his foolish talk and he prayed for his friends who had tried to comfort and instruct him.

Then God did the miraculous! His physical and mental suffering came to an end. God turned his captivity and restored to him twice as much as he had in the beginning.

Let your captivity be turned today and enjoy the fullness of the blessings of your Heavenly Father.

Barbara J. White

Christian Literature & Artwork
A BOLD TRUTH Publication

JOB'S JEOPARDY
Copyright © 2017 by Barbara J. White
ISBN 13: 978-0-9991469-9-6

Healing For the Nations Ministries
PO Box 79126
Corona, California 92877-9998, USA
www.fmint.org ▪ *fmint2010@hotmail.com*

BOLD TRUTH PUBLISHING
(Christian Literature & Artwork)
606 West 41st, Ste. 4
Sand Springs, Oklahoma 74063
www.BoldTruthPublishing.com ▪ *beirep@yahoo.com*

Available from Amazon.com and other retail outlets. Orders by U.S. trade bookstores and wholesalers.

Quantity sales special discounts are available on quantity purchases by corporations, associations, and others. For details, contact the publisher at the address above.

Cover Art & Design by Aaron Jones

Printed in the USA.
11 17   10 9 8 7 6 5 4 3 2 1

Content

Foreword

The psalmist David often integrated his *Psalms* of glorious praise to Jehovah with *"Selah"* or stop, look, listen, and pause and consider what has been said, and apply the teaching personally for self and spiritual improvement.

The author has presented the lessons of Job's Jeopardy, as a *"Selah"* to all believers to learn and consider the experiences of Job and his respect for God's faithfulness, that they too will *"fear God and eschew evil."*

There are three controversies in the book of Job:
- **First:** It is between Heaven and Hell, concerning the earth.
- **Second:** It is between Job and his friends.
- **Third:** It is between Jehovah and Job.

This seems to be a key to the whole book. We see the enthroned and authoritative Jehovah and all angelic beings, both good and bad, compelled to appear before Him and report to Him.

You will be blessed as I was by the author's inspirational statements:

"It is a tremendous risk to live in ignorance of the Word of God.

"Do you feel you are like Job? Then do what Job did—he got himself out of his miserable situation by gaining correct knowledge of the ways and purposes of God.

Foreword

"Secondly, he humbled himself and repented of his foolish talk and he prayed for his friends. God did the miraculous by turning his captivity and restored to him twice as much as he had in the beginning."

In conclusion, *II Corinthians 10:4* states that *"The weapons of our warfare are not carnal but mighty through God..."* The Greek word for warfare is *"stratia"* or what I call *"Heavenly Strategy"*. When you read **Job's Jeopardy** you will be taught by the Holy Spirit the principles of victorious strategy to stir up the anointing within you to fight the good fight of faith.

Dr. Chuck Flynn
Prophetic Trumpet
Orange, California

Chapter 1

What Can We Learn From Job?

You know how we call those blessed (happy) who were steadfast [who endured]. You have heard of the endurance of Job, and you have seen the Lord's [purpose and how He richly blessed him in the] end, inasmuch as the Lord is full of pity and compassion and tenderness and mercy. - James 5:11 AMP

It has not been unusual down through the pages of history to read of godly men and women who have suffered or endured great trials and difficulties. The Old Testament Book of Job has been recorded in our Bible to give us wise instruction, and be profitable in providing information and understanding of where bad things originate and how the godly can overcome in times of predicament, great or small.

The Holy Spirit has a message for each believer in the Book of Job, and the message contained therein is this; there is an eventual end to suffering and calamity if we choose to learn from Job's experiences in light of what the Word of God says concerning suffering.

Much misunderstanding concerning the life of Job has

been promoted and has left those suffering with the idea that they are like Job and must continue to suffer for some mysterious reason. The true message of Job is—one of hope, deliverance, and restoration.

The word *jeopardy* means: exposure to death, loss, injury, danger or risk. [Cite: Webster's New Ideal Dictionary, G & C Merriam Co; 1968.] The word *jeopardy* well defines Job's experience. In fact, Job suffered extensive jeopardy—he experienced great loss, including his ten children, the children's servants, their houses and livestock, then, his health. He was exposed to intense physical pain and injury. His perils have been recorded for a purpose (so that we might not fall into the same trap and think God is the source of our problems). We must not blame Him.

Romans 15:4 tells us that the *things that were written aforetime were written for our learning, that we through patience and comfort of the scriptures might have hope.* We should learn from all that Job went through in order that we might not succumb to the same lack of knowledge, misunderstandings, and mistakes. As New Testament believers, when we lack knowledge of what Jesus did for us at the cross, what He purchased for us with His own precious blood, we will suffer unnecessarily.

My people are destroyed (cut off) for lack of knowledge: because thou hast rejected knowledge, I will also reject thee ... - Hosea 4:6a

What Can We Learn From Job?

Our redemption is complete and eternal. We have a covenant with Almighty God which can never be changed, revoked, or broken *(cf. Ga 3:17)*. The Abrahamic Covenant is in force for all eternity.

A number of unfair conclusions have been directed to God regarding the Book of Job. One being the view that God has to be cruel without regard for His creation because He accepted a challenge from Satan just to prove a point, and indirectly caused an upright man and his family untold suffering.

Another view is that poor, weak God cannot prevent what happened to Job, Satan being too strong. We, and most of enlightened Christendom, of course, in the light of Jesus, His life, and New Testament teaching, would reject both of these arguments.

The Holy Spirit desires to give us understanding and unravel the so-called mysteries of the Book of Job. We trust this book will shed light on the life of Job and help the reader gain a better understanding of how we can learn from the Scriptures and not necessarily go through what others endured. Were not the Scriptures written for our learning? Are they not profitable, providing correction and instruction in righteousness? Isn't it much better to be informed than to live in ignorance of the nature of God and His good and perfect plans for His children? Of course, to be forewarned is to be armed with the accurate knowledge that will enable every believer to overcome the storms of life.

We should all have a clear understanding of who is the *Taker* (thief, killer, destroyer) and Who is the *Giver* of every good and perfect gift, the *Blesser*! Satan *steals, kills, and destroys,* but Jesus gives us a marvelous and abundant life. He is the Blesser!

■ ■ ■

We should learn from all that Job went through in order that we might not succumb to the same lack of knowledge, misunderstandings, and mistakes.

Jesus said, *The thief comes only in order to steal and kill and destroy. I came that they may have and enjoy life, and have it in abundance (to the full, till it overflows). - John 10:10 AMP*

This book does not address the suffering of persecution other than to comment on this kind of suffering as being different from what we are teaching concerning Job's ordeal.

Unfortunately, we as believers are not exempt from persecution in this world; Jesus did not bear it on the cross for us as He did sin, sickness, disease, pain and poverty, and everything associated with the curse. But, He did provide the means whereby we can overcome and triumph in the midst of persecution.

Persecution is a result of God's people living and doing right. It is suffering for the sake of the Gospel and the

What Can We Learn From Job?

Word of God in a Christ-rejecting world. It is not suffering as a result of foolishness or a sinful life. Persecution is an occupational hazard to those who serve God in righteousness and godliness.

Jesus told us we would be persecuted. *Matthew 5:10-12* clearly states why and what we should do when we are persecuted.

> *Blessed are they which are persecuted for righteousness' sake, for theirs is the kingdom of heaven.*
> *Blessed are ye, when men shall revile you, and persecute you, and shall say all manner of evil against you falsely, for my sake.*
> *Rejoice and be exceeding glad: for great is your reward in heaven: for so persecuted they the prophets which were before you.*

Persecution is one of the tools Satan uses to steal the Word of God out of the heart of a believer. If allowed, persecution can cause offense. The result of being offended is that believers will not bring forth the harvest of the Word they had sown into their hearts *(cf. Mr 4:17; Mt 13:21)*. It is simply another way for Satan to steal from us by causing us to get into fear and withdraw from the good fight of faith *(cf. 1 Ti 6:12)*.

Believers must address persecution by binding the enemy and affirming the Words in *Isaiah 54:17 AMP*:

> *But no weapon that is formed against you shall pros-*

per, and every tongue *[word] that shall rise against you in judgment you shall show to be in the wrong. This [peace, righteousness, security, triumph over opposition] is the heritage of the servants of the Lord, [those in whom the ideal Servant of the Lord is reproduced]; this is the righteousness or the vindication which they obtain from Me [this is that which I impart to them as their justification], says the Lord.

* added by the writer

Then we are to do what Jesus said in *Matthew 5:44: Love your enemies, bless them that curse you, do good to them that hate you, and pray for them which despitefully use you, and persecute you.* This behavior on our part brings confusion to Satan and his kingdom, and possibly causes our enemies to be greatly convicted of their sin.

The words in *Romans 8:35 and 37* assure us that persecution cannot separate us from the love of God which is in Christ Jesus our Lord. We are more than conquerors through Him that loves us!

Who shall separate us from the love of Christ? Shall tribulation, or distress, or persecution, or famine, or nakedness, or peril, or sword? ... Nay, in all these things we are more than conquerors through him that loved us.

Chapter 2
The Man from Uz

There was a man in the land of Uz, whose name was Job; and that man was perfect and upright, and one that feared God, and eschewed evil. - Job 1:1

Job was a godly man who stood head and shoulders above all the men of the east. The land of Uz, which has been suggested by some scholars to have been located near Antioch or in northern Mesopotamia, should have been proud of its God-fearing citizen. He displayed integrity and honesty in all of his business and life.

This man's character was impeccable. Job was an upright man in his generation in the sense of being straight and conducting his life and doing right according to the knowledge he possessed. The Bible describes him as being **perfect**, which simply means he was sincere and free of guile and evil intentions. He reverenced God and displayed the deepest honor for Him by turning away and withdrawing himself from evil.

Job has been named along with the greats—Noah and the prophet Daniel, for being a righteous man *(cf. Eze 14: 14, 20).*

These Old Testament men of God were righteous in that—they all walked in the light and knowledge they possessed during the time and dispensation they lived in. Both Noah and Job lived before the giving of the law of Moses, whereas Daniel lived during the dispensation of law; therefore, these three men of God were familiar with offering sacrifices to God, the means whereby men approached God at that time.

What was this man's genealogy and his family line? Did he just happen to be a God-fearing man or did his ancestors sow seeds of faith and the knowledge of God into his life? From whom did he learn this godly lifestyle and manner of life?

As to the time-line, Bible scholars have not come to a conclusion to the dispensation in which Job lived. But there are some clues in the book of Job that help us point to a time: after the flood of Noah and long before Moses.

- In *Job 22:16* Eliphaz refers to the flood as being in the past.

- As the head of his family, Job sacrifices to God as head of his family, a patriarchal practice that stopped with Moses.

- Job's daughters received an inheritance along with his sons *(cf. Job 42:15)*, a patriarchal practice that also stopped with Moses.

- The wealth of Job is determined by flocks rather than

money. This method is consistent with patriarchal times (*cf. Job 1:3; 42:12*).

- The *kesitah* or piece of money mentioned in *Job 42:11* belongs to patriarchal times.

- The musical instruments (organ, harp, and timbrel) are all instruments of early *Genesis*.

- Job made a reference to Adam in *Job 31:33*. He said he did not cover his transgression as Adam did in the garden of Eden. Was Job alive during Adam's lifetime? Or was the knowledge of the fall of man and original sin passed down to him through writings or orally through the patriarchs?

- Job lived long enough to birth two families of ten children and raise them to adulthood, then lived another 140 years. He could have lived 200 years and possibly longer. *[Source: The Amazing Bible Timeline]*

Job was so blessed that he was considered the greatest of all the men of the east. He and his wife were fruitful and God had blessed them with seven sons and three daughters. Job was indeed a very rich man. God had made him rich as we read in *Job 1:3 and 10*. This can be attributed to his godly character and his reverence for God.

His substance also was seven thousand sheep, and

three thousand camels, and five hundred yoke of oxen, and five hundred she asses, and a very great household; so that this man was the greatest of all the men of the east. - Job 1:3

It is not certain whether Moses wrote the Book of Job or if Job recorded it himself. However, the Book of Job is the oldest book in our Bible and is inspired by the Holy Spirit for our benefit and learning. Job requested to have his experience written in a book *(cf. Job 19:23-24).* We are glad that his request was granted—it is for our profit and wisdom! According to theologians Job was about 70 years of age when these devastating adversities happened to him, his family, and possessions.

The adversary (Satan) had been thrown out of Heaven. *Revelations 12:4 and 9* tell us of his great fall and how he took with him a third of the angels in Heaven. Then he had the audacity to show up at Heaven's worship services! He was not legally banned from Heaven until Jesus died, rose again, and ascended back to the Father in Heaven.

When Satan came and joined himself with the angels of God in Heaven as they worshipped before the throne, Job was not aware at that time what was happening. In fact, in the Old Testament, people knew very little of the activity of Satan and demons. If they had possessed knowledge of Satan they would not have had the authority and power to deal with him as believers do today. We now have the Name of Jesus, the Word of God, the power of the Holy Spirit, and the Blood of Jesus to overcome and enforce the defeat of all the power of the devil and demons *(cf. Re 12:11; Lu 10:19)*.

Through lack of knowledge Old Testament people would attribute everything good or bad as coming from God. This was the prevailing Hebrew attitude at that time, and even today it is common in the Church to believe this. There is a difference between God **commissioning or causing** something and God **allowing or permitting** something to happen. As a result of free will given to man in the beginning and his decision to disobey God, He had to allow many evil things to happen because man allowed them.

Freedom of choice is an awesome responsibility on the part of man. On the other hand, it is a tremendous blessing because we can choose God, and no demon can stop us. We have the authority to choose life and all the blessings that come with this kind of everlasting life. Choosing the God kind of life means rejecting sin and its evil effects. When man fell in the Garden of Eden Satan became the god of this world *(cf. 2 Co 4:4)*. To the believer he is not our god any longer, Jesus is our Lord and we have passed from death unto life, praise God!

During these particular occasions in Job's life Satan was an intruder in Heaven. He 'gate crashed' into the very presence of God—no invitation had been sent to him. But no longer can he enter Heaven. Jesus whipped him, spoiled him and his principalities, defeating them at the cross through His shed blood *(cf. Col 2:15)*. The Blood of Jesus cleansed the contamination Satan brought into Heaven *(cf. Heb 9: 22-23)*. Jesus said in *Luke 10:18* that *He beheld Satan as lightening fall from Heaven.*

When God confronted Satan, this arrogant intruder, He addressed him with this question: *"Where did you come from?"* His answer was, *"From going to and fro in the earth, and from walking up and down in it." (cf. Job 1:7)*

In Chapter 1 God poses a question to Satan, *"Have you considered my servant Job—there is none like him in the earth, a perfect and an upright man, one that fears Me, and departs from evil?"*

The dialogue continues with questions and observations from Satan directed to God:

"Does Job fear [reverence] You for nothing?" It seems Satan was saying to the Lord, *"Would Job still reverence You even if he had nothing?"* This is a big question for many of today's materialistic Christians. We have known of preachers who wouldn't preach unless they were guaranteed a huge amount of money.

Then Satan proceeds to say to God, *"Have you not put a hedge about him and about his house and about all that he has on every side? You have conferred prosperity and happiness upon*

12

him in the work of his hands, and his possessions have in-creased in the land." Observe how Satan knows those who are blessed of the Lord. Then Satan audaciously challenges God by saying: *"But put forth Your hand now and touch all that he has, and he will curse You to Your face." (cf. Job 1:11)*

Verse 12 is so enlightening! The Lord responds to Satan with these significant Words, *"Behold all that he has is in your power."* Now let's consider just what the Lord was saying. This is one of the key truths to understanding the Book of Job.

Nowhere in the New Testament does it say that believers are in Satan's power or authority. Satan is now under our feet *(cf. Eph 1:19-23)*. We now, as believers, have all *author-ity over all the power of the enemy and nothing shall by any means hurt us (cf. Lu 10:19)*. Jesus spoke this right after say-ing He saw *Satan fall as lightening from Heaven (v 18)*.

■ ■ ■

...we can choose God, and no demon can stop us. We have the authority to choose life and all the blessings that come with this kind of everlasting life.

In the New Testament you cannot find anywhere that it says that the Body of Christ has been put into Satan's hands. It says quite the opposite. Satan is now under our feet, under our authority. If you as a Christian find yourself in Satan's hand there is the possibility that you gave place to him. The Apostle Paul says we as believers are to *leave no such room or foothold for the devil [give no opportunity to him] (cf. Eph 4:27 AMP)*. Uninformed Job couldn't and didn't do that. He had no idea what had been going on in Heaven between God and Satan.

Now God said that everything Job has at this time is in Satan's power or authority. How did this happen? Satan had just said God had hedged him about on all sides. Which was initially true but somehow the hedge got broken-down. How, you say, did this happen?

An interesting Scripture, *Ecclesiastes 10:8* gives us a clue.

> *He that diggeth a pit shall fall into it; and whoso breaketh an hedge; a serpent shall bite him.*

God doesn't tear down the hedge of protection He provides for us; He is not a thief or a destroyer. But Satan can break through a broken-down hedge. So how did Job's hedge get broken-down? It was the **fear factor**! How do we know?

We go to *Job 3:25, For the thing which I greatly feared is come upon me, and that which I was afraid of is come unto me*. Everything that happened to him was a result of his great fear. His fear broke down his hedge of protection. That is the same way Satan works today; he has no new tricks, he simply works the same way he always has. But we should

14

be wiser as a result of the knowledge of the Word of God.

Satan, that old Serpent, the Devil, bit Job and devoured his children, his children's servants, his livestock, and his health. But it was only for a season until Job got his thinking straightened out and made some adjustments.

Another verse that brings revelation and enlightenment to Job's jeopardy is found in *Proverbs 26:2*.

> *As the bird by wandering, as the swallow by flying, so the curse causeless shall not come.*

The message is this: there is always a cause or reason for the curse coming. The cause in Job's case was a lack of knowledge, which in turn—produced great fear.

Job could not access the Book of Isaiah, for it was not to be written for many years. He could not read these comforting words, which apply to all believers today.

> *You shall establish yourself in righteousness (rightness, in conformity with God's will and order): you shall be far from even the thought of oppression or destruction, for you shall not fear, and from terror, for it shall not come near you. Behold, they may gather together and stir up strife, but it is not from Me. Whoever stirs up strife against you shall fall and surrender to you. - Isaiah 54:14-15*

Notice what God says concerning oppression, destruction, fear and terror—they are not from Him! If these were the only verses in the Bible we knew, without a doubt we would know God is not the source or cause of such dreadful actions. But we have many Scriptures available to us to show us the absolute goodness of our Heavenly Father.

Chapter 3

The Fear Factor

I n spite of Job's piety and reverence for God he fell short in the area of exercising faith for his children and their protection as well as his own health and safety. His children should have been proud to have such a godly father whose affluence provided well for them. Did they really live in sin? Or was Job full of fear that they were doing wrong? We don't know exactly.

When Job's children came together regularly to feast and celebrate in their houses he was afraid they might have sinned and cursed God in their hearts. Job's sons and daughters would celebrate, each on "his day", meaning they would have at least ten birthday parties a year in their respective homes. Job repeatedly offered burnt of-ferings to God on their behalf. Did Job time and again offer sacrifices on behalf of his family in faith or was he motivated by fear?

The answer to this question comes in *Job 3:25-26*:

> *For the thing which I greatly feared is come upon me, and that which I was afraid of is come unto me. I was*

not in safety, neither had I rest, neither was I quiet; yet trouble came.

This is again confirmed in other verses in this book.

I am afraid of all my complaint. - Job 9:2

Even when I remember I am afraid, and trembling taketh hold on my flesh. - Job 21:6

Therefore am I troubled at his presence: when I consider I am afraid of him [God]. - Job 23:15

Tormenting fear always opens the door for Satan to step in and bring destruction. Jesus told us Satan had come to steal, kill and destroy *(cf. Joh 10:10)*. But Job didn't know this. Lack of knowledge brought fear and fear turned into great fear, and great fear produced a devastating harvest. Fear provided an entrance for Satan to do his diabolical work upon Job, his family, and his possessions.

We know Job was not operating in faith because fear cancels out faith and as a result of fear he was not in rest. Faith is a rest *(cf. Heb 4:3)*. This rest means you have peace in your heart and mind. You are not anxious and worried about anything *(cf. Php 4: 6-7)*.

Job couldn't turn to *Psalms 91* and affirm his faith with these words:

The Fear Factor

I will say of the Lord, He is my refuge and my fortress, my God; in him will I trust ... Thou shalt not be afraid for the terror by night, nor for the arrow that flieth by day ... nor for the pestilence that walketh in darkness; nor for the destruction that wasteth at noonday ... A thousand shall fall at thy side, and ten thousand at thy right hand; but it shall not come nigh thee ...

Job didn't have *Luke 10:19* to act upon. His knowledge of the authority of the believer was unknown to him. Through **great fear** Job had placed himself in a very vulnerable position for Satan to do his destructive work. We as New Testament believers are told to firstly, submit ourselves to God, then to resist the devil and he would flee from us *(cf. Jas 4:7)*. Ignorance of God's Word is a terrible handicap. We must allow the fact that Satan's activities in the unseen sphere were unknown to most of God's people in the Old Testament because they had no means to combat him until the cross and resurrection of Jesus gave us authority over Satan and demons.

First, the Sabeans came and took away Job's oxen and asses and slew the servants, except for the one who escaped to tell him.

Then another servant came reporting of further loss. This time the 7,000 sheep were consumed in a fire (perhaps caused by lightening) as well as destroying the servants.

Before Job could take it all in, another servant who had escaped came reporting how the Chaldeans had carried away his 3,000 camels and slain the servants. While this servant was speaking another servant came bearing the bad news that Job's sons and daughters were destroyed by a hurricane or tornado. Their home had fallen on them and the servants, killing them all.

Now Job didn't lose his own house, servants, or his wife *(cf. Job 19:15-19)*. But his servants did turn against him; His wife scorned him and wanted him to curse God and die! Job's response to his wife's words were to the affect that she was speaking as one of the foolish women. Job's ignorance of the nature of God is revealed when he asked, *What? shall we not receive good at the hand of God, and shall we not receive evil? (cf. Job 2:10)*

■ ■ ■

Tormenting fear always opens the door for Satan to step in and bring destruction.

Great calamity had visited Job that day! He arose in his distress and overwhelming shock, ripped his mantle, shaved his head, and fell down upon the ground and worshipped God.

Now his first mistake was not to worship God and bless His Name, but it was to claim that the Lord had taken away his family, their homes, his livestock, and his children's servants.

The Fear Factor

... the Lord gave, and the Lord hath taken away, blessed be the name of the Lord. -- Job 1:21

The words **the Lord gave** are true, for God had given Job all that he had, but the words, **the Lord hath taken away,** are not a statement of truth. These words have been spoken time and again by sincere people in the time of death, sickness, calamity, and other evils.

Even in today's Christian world believers quote Job's words as if they were God's truth; while it is absolutely true that Job quoted these words, the latter part of this declaration is not a true statement. These are not the words of God, but the words of a man who lacked knowledge of the origin and source of evil.

One lesson we must learn from Job is that we are never to blame God for evil in the earth! Even James, a New Testament pastor, tells us:

Let no man say when he is tempted [tried], I am tempted [tried] of God: for God cannot be tempted [tried] with evil, neither tempteth [tries] he any man [with evil]... Every good gift and every perfect gift is from above, and cometh down from the Father of lights, with whom is no variableness, neither shadow of turning. - James 1:13, 17

Jesus told us to pray, *Deliver us from evil*—not deliver us from

JOB'S JEOPARDY

God *(cf. Mt 6:13)*. The word *evil* here means: **the evil one.**

Again Satan presented himself before the Lord *(cf. Job 2:1)*. On this second occasion God asks him where he has been and brings up the subject of Job. But this time Satan's evil intent was to destroy Job and he challenged God to destroy his body and then Job would curse Him to His face. A second time the Lord said unto Satan, *"Behold he is in thine hand; but save his life." (cf. Job 2:4-6)* Satan's sphere of destruction was limited. He can only go so far towards those who truly love God.

> *There hath no temptation taken you but such as is common to man: but God is faithful, who will not suffer you to be tempted above that ye are able; but will with the temptation also make a way to escape, that ye may be able to bear it. - 1 Corinthians 10:13*

The following verses tell us what Satan (not God) did to Job's body. Satan smote Job with sore boils from the sole of his foot to the crown of his head *(cf. Job 2:7)*. Today much sickness and disease is directly from Satan and demons.

So great was the agony of this attack in Job's body that he had to scrape himself with a piece of broken pottery to get some relief. His place of escape was down among the ashes. Not too becoming for such a greatly honored man in his community. Do you see how far Satan will bring a man down if he is permitted? This portion of Scripture gives us great insight into the origin of sickness and disease.

Job's boils and pain did not come from God in Heaven, (for God has no sickness to give), but from Satan himself! He hasn't changed today, he is still putting sickness, disease, and pain on people's bodies. The tragedy is that so often people believe the diabolical work of sickness and disease is sent from God to teach and perfect them.

When Job's wife saw the great loss of their wealth, their children, and the loss of Job's health, she provoked him to curse God and then die. But up to this time Job held fast to his integrity and refused to renounce God or charge Him foolishly. So often we hear of people who love God with all their heart and soul and live in the light they have, yet suffer so much at the hand of Satan. Job is one such example.

■ ■ ■

One lesson we must learn from Job is that we are never to blame God for evil in the earth!

Loving God in itself will not bring a believer deliverance from the attacks of the enemy. It is vital for believers to walk in love and to be filled with information and revelation knowledge of the Word of God about 'how to walk in their authority here on the earth'.

Our faith works by love *(cf. Ga 5:6)*. Sickness, disease, and pain are real unholy enemies that Jesus destroyed with the stripes He bore, even before He went to the cross *(cf. Isa 53:4-5)*, yet so many Christians are suffering in this way. Why, you may ask?

Lack of knowledge of what Jesus obtained for us will hold any believer in bondage and Satan will take advantage of their ignorance. A believer's faith will rise no higher than the revelation knowledge they have of the Word of God.

Once knowledge has been obtained there is the next step, and that is to act on what you believe in your heart. Acting on the Word and speaking in agreement with the Word brings Bible results; deliverance, and freedom from the curse!

Chapter 4

Ignorant Accusations

Even Job's integrity didn't deliver him from his jeopardy and tormenting nightmare. Satan cruelly terrorized him and he thought God was responsible for it.

We read throughout this book that Job spoke ignorantly many times of God's ways. His ignorant accusations should teach us to never say the same things. You can read these throughout *Chapters 1 through 30.*

We will list some of these for our information and understanding:

1. *The Lord hath taken away. - Job 1:21*

2. *The arrows of the Almighty are within me, the poison whereof drinketh up my spirit: the terrors of God do set themselves in array against me. - Job 6:4*

3. *He (God) breaketh me with tempest, and multiplieth my wounds without cause. - Job 9:17-18*

4. *Does it seem good to You that You should oppress, that*

you should despise and reject the work of Your hands?
- Job 10:3 AMP

5. *Though He slay me, yet will I trust in Him. - Job 13:15*

6. *Why do You hide Your face [as if offended] and alienate me as if I were Your enemy?. - Job 13:24 AMP*

7. *Thou destroyest the hope of man. - Job 14:19*

8. *But now he hath made me weary. - Job 16:7*

9. *God hath delivered me to the ungodly. - Job 16:11*

10. *Know now that God hath overthrown me. - Job 19:6*

11. *Behold, I cry out of wrong, but I am not heard.*
- Job 19:7

12. *He has stripped me of my glory, and taken the crown from my head. He has destroyed me on every side.*
- Job 19:9-10

13. *He hath also kindled His wrath against me. - Job 19:11*

14. *The Almighty troubleth me. - Job 23:16*

15. *Because he hath loosed my cord and afflicted me.*
- Job 30:11

16. *He hath cast me into the mire, and I am become like dust and ashes. - Job 30:19*

17. *I cry unto thee and thou dost not hear me. - Job 30:20*

18. *Thou art become cruel to me; with thy strong hand thou opposest thyself against me. - Job 30:21*

19. *Thou liftest me up to the wind; thou causest me to ride upon it, and dissolvest my substance. - Job 30:22*

Every statement made by Job in these verses is untrue, for it was Satan who took away his substance, harrowed him, and did all the other wicked things to Job. It was after his three friends came and tried to counsel him with their carnal reasoning, and his unbearable suffering continued, that he began to sin with his words.

■ ■ ■

A believer's faith will rise no higher than the revelation knowledge they have of the Word of God.

Historians and Bible chronologists tell us that Job suffered for about nine months before his captivity was turned.

During this great trial Job lifted his voice with a prophetic word that has been a blessing to believers and we must give credit to this inspired word:

27

For I know that my redeemer liveth, and that he shall stand at the latter day upon the earth: And though after my skin worms destroy this body, yet in my flesh shall I see God: Whom I shall see for myself, and mine eyes shall behold and not another, though my reins be consumed within me. - Job 19:25-27

Job knew that one day he would actually see God, his eyes would behold Him, His Redeemer! The Amplified Bible states *verse 25* this way:

For I know that my Redeemer and Vindicator lives, and at last He (the last One) will stand upon the earth.

Yes, our Redeemer is our Vindicator and He is alive, the same yesterday, today and forever, the ever present One, the Lord Jesus Christ, who has redeemed us with His own precious blood from all the power of Satan and his demons! We shall all behold Him one day—even face to face! *(cf. Re 22:3-4)*

The Lord became Job's Redeemer and Deliverer! It was given to him on credit, as it were, before the cross and the penalty for sin, sickness, disease, poverty, and all the effects of the curse were paid for. Believers today do not receive on credit, they receive by faith what has already been provided for them in Jesus Christ. The price has been paid in full for our complete redemption from the curse of sin, sickness, disease, pain, and poverty.

Ignorant Accusations

Christ hath redeemed us from the curse of the law being made a curse for us: for it is written, Cursed is everyone that hangeth on a tree:

That the blessing of Abraham might come on the Gentiles through Jesus Christ; that we might receive the promise of the Spirit through faith. - Galatians 3: 13-14

JOB'S JEOPARDY

Chapter 5

Comfort or Condemn?

Job had three friends that did their best to bring comfort to him in his time of misery and pain. At first they didn't recognize him due to the distressing boils all over his body. They joined him on the ground for the first seven days and nights and wept as they tore their clothes and sprinkled dust upon their heads. They were tongue-tied for seven days, unable to speak a word to Job seeing his excruciating pain and grief.

Job was the first to speak and he proceeded to speak curses on the day he was born. He wished he had never been born or grown into manhood. At this point he makes the confession that he *greatly feared* all that had come on him.

At the end of the seven days Eliphaz, the Temanite was the first to speak. His many words were of condemnation. *"Job, you are reaping what you have sown! You are suffering these calamities so you must be wicked."* And on and on he labored the point. Not much comfort to a hurting man!

Job's response to Eliphaz was that he accused God of being his enemy, asking Him to destroy him. In fact, he longs to

31

die. Job goes on to reprove his friends for their lack of understanding and asks them to show pity on him.

The next friend to join in the discourse was Bildad, the Shuhite. He accused Job of being wicked, otherwise he would not be suffering and his children would not have been cast away. And besides that, he rebuked him for being a hypocrite!

All these accusations from his so-called friends prompted Job to complain against God further. It brought more confusion to his mind. Job thought, *If there was only a mediator between me and God, one that might lay his hand upon us both. (Job 9:33 paraphrased).* His heart was crying out for the One Who was to come to be the Mediator between God and men, the man Christ Jesus.

> *For there is one mediator between God and men, the man Christ Jesus. - 1 Timothy 2:5*

On one hand Job would pray to God for help and then he would accuse God of increasing His wrath upon him. The perplexity continued in Job's mind.

Zophar, the Naamathite contributes to the discourse by adding insult to injury by saying that Job deserved much more suffering and reaping for his iniquity *(cf. Job 11:5-6)*. He tries to assure Job that if he would just stop sinning God would bless him.

Comfort or Condemn?

What man, who is suffering indescribable pain as Job, needs this kind of condemnation? Their words had made him feel inferior to them. In Job's indignation of their censure he tells them that they are lying and they have only provoked him to speak things he did not wish to say.

In *Job 13: 5* Job utters an amusing statement to these three men: *Oh, that you would hold your peace (be quiet)—it would prove that you had some sense! (paraphrased).*

On and on the conversations proceed between these three men and Job. He had to tell them that they are all *miserable comforters (cf. Job 16:2), vexing his soul and breaking him with words (cf. Job 19:2).* They continued to taunt him by speaking doom and gloom over his life.

■ ■ ■

Lack of knowledge of what Jesus obtained for us will hold any believer in bondage and Satan will take advantage of their ignorance.

Eliphaz told Job to pay his vows, then God will bless him: *Thou shalt also decree a thing, and it shall be established unto thee and the light shall shine upon thy ways.*
- *Job 22:28*

All these words caused Job to philosophize and reason with

his mind as to why he was suffering as he was. In *Chapter 29*, Job grieves over his past when God had preserved him—his children were with him and he enjoyed great prosperity as a result of God's blessings. He continues to recall all the good works he had performed in the city. Job recounts the times he helped the poor and the fatherless; when he was eyes to the blind and feet to the lame.

Chapter 31 tells how Job tried to justify himself by making certain declarations:

> *I am not guilty of lusting after a woman, being dishonest, committing adultery, injustice, or being inhumane toward the poor, the widow or the fatherless. I have not made gold my hope nor rejoiced in my great wealth. I have not been guilty of idolatry, such as worshipping the sun or moon. I would not speak a curse on those who hate me. I was always ready to welcome the stranger in my house. I did not cover my transgressions as Adam did by hiding my iniquity. I have not been guilty of fraud by eating the fruit of the field and not paying for them.*

At this point Eliphaz, Bildad and Zophar stopped talking to Job because they considered he was righteous in his own eyes.

There was another man, Elihu, younger than the others, who was present listening to all the arguments between the three men and Job. Because of his youth he was timid in coming forward and giving his opinion to Job and the others. But he finally gained confidence to speak up!

Elihu was indignant against Job because he justified himself rather than acknowledging God had justified him. He expressed his anger towards the three miserable comforters because they were unable to give an answer to Job or show his real error. These three had declared Job to be wrong and responsible for his own affliction *(cf. Job 32:1-3)*.

Now Job, Elihu went on to say, *these are the errors you have committed, as I see it. You have said, 'I am clean without transgression.'*

You have said you are innocent, [Job did not use the word 'innocent' but it is implied in his statements]. *You go on to say that you have no iniquity in you; and God finds occasions against me and counts me as His enemy. He puts my feet in the stocks and marks all my paths. In fact, you strive against God (cf. Job 33).*

Now Job had spent a lot of time dwelling on himself—his own sincerity and righteousness, feeling he was innocent of any sin.

One thing that we must give credit to Elihu is that he defended God and praised him for His mighty strength, wisdom, and righteousness *(cf. Job 36:5-33)*. In *Chapter 37* Job is advised by Elihu to consider the power and works of God and not presume to be wiser than God. Take note of *Job 37:23*.

Touching the Almighty, we cannot find him out: he is excellent in power, and in judgment, and in plenty of justice: he will not afflict.

Take note of Elihu's words: *he will not afflict.* This is one revelation Job needed to hear and know personally. *God does not afflict!*

Then the Lord speaks to Job out of the whirlwind. It was time for Job to listen to the Almighty—men had tried to counsel him out of their limited knowledge and soulish realm. It was time for God to speak and bring truth to bear on this man's life and experiences. Light was about to shine into Job's mind and heart.

Chapter 6
Recovery Time

When Almighty God speaks man should listen! The first question God posed to Job was:

Who is this that darkeneth counsel by words without knowledge? - Job 38:2

This is the first of many questions God asked Job as recorded in *Chapters 38-42.* Job had uttered many accusations—murmuring and complaining against the Almighty God.

Even Elihu told Job that he opened his mouth in vain and multiplied words without knowledge *(cf. Job 35:16).* Numerous times Job had put his foot in his mouth.

God continues questioning Job concerning creation. *Where were you Job when I laid the foundations of the earth? ... When the morning stars sang together, and all the sons of God shouted for joy?*

And on and on the questions concerning creation, including the inanimate and animate, are presented to Job by

God. Then comes a question on a very personal level:

Shall he that contendeth with the Almighty instruct him? He that reproveth God, let him answer it. ...Gird up thy loins now like a man: I will demand of thee, and declare thou unto me. Wilt thou also disannul my judgment? Wilt thou condemn me, that thou mayest be righteous? Hast thou an arm like God? Or canst thou thunder with a voice like him? - Job 40:2, 6-9

Did Job Release Anger?

During Job's outbursts, both to his friends and towards God, it seems he had an immense anger problem. We know from our study that he definitely was ignorant of the ways and will of God.

We must remember that Job suffered a huge loss. It was devastating for a man to lose ten children, houses, property, his wealth and his livelihood. Everything he had, including his earthly security, had been stripped away by Satan. On top of that he lost his health and suffered unimaginable pain in his body. The loss was not just physical pain but strong emotional pain. The human reaction of loss is to become angry to some degree. It varies from person to person. In *Galatians 5:20* one of the **works of the flesh** is **anger** which will manifest in our emotions and words.

I can empathize with Job to some degree. Before my husband went to be with the Lord I became angry. It was never anger towards God because I know He is always good. My anger manifested because of the sense of loss and grief long before he actually went to heaven. The pain of loss was almost unbearable at times, I thank God he sent me wonderful Christians friends who helped me recognize my anger problem. I was able to repent and deal with the strong negative emotions with the help of the Word of God and praying in the Holy Spirit. Thank God, today I am free of anger.

I do believe some of Job's outbursts and accusations were based on anger. His flesh was overwhelmed by the devastating circumstances he was going through. His anger didn't automatically go away, he had to acknowledge it and repent before his restoration came. God in His great grace and mercy doubled everything Job had lost. What a beautiful example of the grace of God.

Words of Correction

Here God's Words of correction and rebuke pointed out Job's sins, namely:

1. You contended with the Almighty in order to instruct Him. *(cf. Job 40:2)*

2. You reproved God. *(cf. Job 40:2)*

3. You disannulled God's judgment.   *(cf. Job 40:8)*

4. You condemned God to make yourself righteous.
     (cf. Job 40:8)

5. You hid counsel without knowledge.   *(cf. Job 42:3)*

6. You uttered what you did not understand. *(cf. Job 42:3)*

How did God administer correction and discipline to Job? He did it with Words—His Words, which are spirit and life *(cf. Joh 6:63)*. He did not use sickness, disease, accidents, and evil calamities as so many believe today.

In the New Testament God operates in exactly the same way, He brings correction and reproof and teaches His people with His Word and the Holy Spirit. Jesus told us that the Holy Spirit is the Teacher of the Church in *John 14:26*, and that the Holy Spirit would guide us into all truth *(cf. Joh 16:13)*.

In *1 Timothy 3:16-17* Paul tells us;

> *All scripture is given by inspiration of God, and is profitable for doctrine, for reproof, for correction, for instruction in righteousness: That the man of God may be perfect, thoroughly furnished unto all good works.*

As we look at *Chapter 42* we read of Job's reply to God. At

40

last he was being enlightened and humbly declares how he
had uttered things that he did not understand:

> *Therefore have I uttered that I understood not; things*
> *too wonderful for me, which I knew not ... I have*
> *heard of thee by the hearing of the ear: but now mine*
> *eye seeth thee. Wherefore I abhor myself, and repent*
> *in dust and ashes. - Job 42:3-6*

Job's spiritual eyes were open at last. His word, *now mine
eye seeth thee* may have indicated that his physical eyes
saw the Lord too, we don't know for certain.

■ ■ ■

How did God administer correction and discipline to Job? He did it with Words— His Words, which are spirit and life.

So now we find Job humbly repenting of his sins. Now it
was time for God to deal with Job's three friends. God ad-
dresses Eliphaz and his two friends rebuking them with
these words:

> *My wrath is kindled against thee and thy two friends:*
> *for ye have not spoken of me the thing that is right, as*
> *my servant Job hath. - Job 42:7*

The next instruction from God to the three comforters
was to take seven bullocks and seven rams and go to Job

and offer up for yourselves a burnt offering. Then my servant Job will pray for you. I will accept his prayer on your behalf. And so these three men did as the Lord commanded—the Lord also accepting Job. *(cf. Job 42:8-9)*

The time of Job's release from his **captivity** was at hand. It is important to note what God called Job's calamity. He called his sickness, loss of family, livestock, houses, and possessions a **captivity**, not a blessing. Modern Christians are guilty of false accusations when they say God did the evil things to them when it was Satan's work.

Jesus called sickness a **bondage** in *Luke 13:11-16*. He loosed this woman, a daughter of Abraham, from the bondage of sickness (spirit of infirmity) and immediately she was made straight and glorified God. Sickness never glorifies God—healing always does!

The Lord turned Job's captivity from Satan when he prayed for his friends. Satan's attacks were completely defeated. That means God healed Job's body and restored twice as much as he had in the beginning. Twice as many sheep, camels, oxen and asses. Besides that he had seven more sons and three beautiful daughters.

And the Lord turned the captivity of Job, when he prayed for his friends: also the Lord gave Job twice as much as he had before. - Job 42:10

Recovery Time

Nothing is mentioned of his wife but we wonder if she repented of her rash statement in the beginning asking Job to curse God and die. If she did she would have been happy to have Job home once again a healthy and prosperous man, not to mention she and Job would enjoy parenting ten more children.

Job's family and friends came to him in his house, once again enjoying his hospitality as they ate together and comforted him. Each one blessed him with a piece of money and an ear ring of gold. These gifts were part of his restoration too.

Job's life was extended and he lived one hundred and forty years after this great trial of approximately nine months duration. He lived in the blessing of the Lord and saw four generations. He was a man satisfied with his life and the number of his days. His children all received an inheritance from their father.

JOB'S JEOPARDY

Chapter 7

Don't Jeopardize Your Life

I t is a tremendous risk to live in ignorance of the Word of God. Your life can be exposed to loss of health, accidents, injury and you can even experience premature death. Satan will certainly take advantage of a believer's lack of knowledge as we can readily see in the life of Job.

The Apostle Paul admonished us to *not be ignorant of Satan's wiles and intentions (cf. 2 Co 2:11 AMP)*. Knowledge of the Word of God acted upon will keep Satan from getting the advantage over us.

There seems to be a parallel between the life of Job and believers today in the Church. So many are suffering unnecessarily through a lack of knowledge of the Word of God. *Hosea 4:6* says, *My people are destroyed for lack of knowledge...* It is one thing to hear the Word and receive it as the Truth, and it is quite another to reject what you hear as the people did in Hosea's day. Watch that you do not reject the Truth.

Job had no Bible to read, he only possessed knowledge of

God and His nature through word of mouth passed down to him by his family or other God-fearing people living at that time. Their knowledge was limited, especially knowing about Satan, the Adversary, and his destructive works. Thank God we know through the Word of God that Jesus was *manifested to destroy the works of the devil (cf. 1 Jo 3:8).* We also know that we overcome all trials and problems by exercising faith in what the Blood of Jesus has done for us personally, and the words of our confession [the Word of God] coming from our spirit *(cf. Re 12:11).*

What can we learn from Job's experiences?

The first thing is to find out how to not live in fear! When we know by personal revelation that *God has not given us the spirit of fear, but of power, and of love, and of a sound mind (cf. 2 Ti 1:7),* we can stand firm against any thoughts of fear that might assail us.

God has given us **the spirit of faith** *(cf. 2 Co 4:13)* that we might speak His word with assurance and confidence. None of us can rise higher in our faith than the knowledge of the Word of God we possess in our spirit, combined with a renewed mind. A renewed mind is such a valuable asset and most necessary in fighting the good fight of faith *(cf. Ro 12:2).*

Fear is not from God for fear has great torment *(cf. 1 Jo 4:16)* and will draw us away from the promises of God and

46

negate our faith. Fear and faith cannot operate in the life of a believer at the same time. We choose one or the other. By choosing to live by faith in the Word of God we choose not to live in fear.

Fear can be dealt with in the same way we choose not to yield to any temptation to sin. Fear does not please God—faith always does *(cf. Heb 11:6)*. When thoughts of fear come to you rebuke them in the Name of Jesus and replace them with faith-filled thoughts and speak God's Word boldly. The Word of God is your defense and will strengthen you to continue believing God, no matter what you may be facing, seeing, or feeling.

I personally know of a dear Christian sister who allowed fear to overcome her in the area of sickness and she died far before her time. She feared she would not live past a certain age because her mother had died young.

Not conquering this fear brought her to an untimely death. Suddenly the enemy attacked her body with a life threatening disease and she went to be with the Lord far sooner than she should have. How many God-fearing believers who loved the Lord with all their heart have gone to heaven before they completed the call on their lives through fear?

Yes, there is much to be learned from the life and experiences of Job. Looking at what James writes about him and applying it to our lives can save us much misery and grief.

You know we call those blessed [happy, spiritually prosperous, favored by God] who were steadfast and endured [difficult circumstances]. You have heard of the patient endurance of Job and you have seen the Lord's outcome [how He richly blessed Job]. The Lord is full of compassion and is merciful. - James 5:11 AMP

In all his trials Job did not give up on the faithfulness of God, even though he thought for a season God was responsible for all his troubles. When he got his thinking straightened out, repented of his ignorance and self-righteousness, and humbly prayed for his misinformed friends, God turned his captivity and restored twice as much as he had before. What a jubilant day it was for Job.

■ ■ ■

Thank God we know through the Word of God that *Jesus was manifested to destroy the works of the devil.*

We see the Lord's purpose being worked out for Job. God's plan and purpose was to deliver him from his captivity to Satan and richly bless Him in the end. How full of mercy and compassion our God is. He never changes! For the next 140 years of Job's life we do not read that he suffered such insidious attacks from Satan.

The knowledge of the truth he acted upon had made him free and God will make and keep us free too. *And you shall know the truth, and the truth shall make you free. (cf. Joh 8:32)* We must stand fast in faith in that glorious liberty of the children of God *(cf. Ga 5:1).*

Jesus told us that in the world we would have trials, troubles, distress, and frustration. None of us are exempt from them *(cf. Joh 16:33).* God is definitely not the author of them and He doesn't commission the trials. But because we are living in a hostile environment dominated by the god of this world, we need to know what God has provided for us in Jesus [the full armor of God in *Ephesians 6*] and how to face and overcome every attack. The Lord has provided a way of deliverance for His people. Jesus said:

> *... but be of good cheer [take courage; be confident, certain, undaunted]! For I have overcome the world. [I have deprived it of power to harm you and have conquered it for you] - John 16:33 AMP*

Jesus also told us in *Matthew 6:13* that we are to pray that we be not led into temptation. This word **temptation** means "trials and tests".

Faith is the victory that overcomes the world [problems we face in this world] *(cf. 1 Joh 5:4).* Our faith is undergirded by the force of patience residing in our spirit. But we have the responsibility of letting patience [endurance] have her perfect work in us so that we may be people perfectly developed, lacking in nothing *(cf. Jas 1:4 AMP).* Read my

49

book, *Let Patience Work For You* to gain further teaching and understanding on the subject of patience.

James reminds us in *James 1:12*:

> *Blessed is the man that endureth temptation [trials and troubles]: for when he is tried, he shall receive the crown of life, which the Lord hath promised to them that love Him.*

You may ask, *"When trouble comes how am I to deal with it?"*

I'm so glad you asked!

1. Recognize that Satan is the author of all evil in this world *(cf. Joh 10:10)*.

2. Judge yourself by examining your words, attitudes or actions that might have left a gap in your hedge of protection *(cf. 1 Co 11:28-31)*. There may be no gap in your hedge, it may be a direct onslaught of Satan. Attacks can come because we are living and doing right. Job was living right, except for lack of knowledge and allowing fear.

3. Don't allow any condemnation. God does not condemn His children, He convicts or convinces them through His Word and the Holy Spirit how to make any necessary adjustments *(cf. Ro 8:1).*

4. Repent if necessary *(cf. 1 Jo 1:9)* and receive cleansing and live and talk with the confidence that God is delivering you.

5. Ask God for wisdom *(cf. Jas 1:5).*

6. Submit yourself to God *(cf. Jas 4:7).*

7. *Resist the Devil and he will flee from you (cf. Jas 4:7).*

8. If you are afflicted—or troubled in any way, pray *(cf. Jas 5:13).*

9. If you are sick, do what *James 5:14* says. *Call for the elders to pray for you, anointing you with oil in the Name of the Lord, and the prayer of faith shall save (heal) you, (cf. Jas 5:14-15).* Or have another believer lay hands on you *(cf. Mr 16:16-18),* or pray yourself and believe you receive *(cf. Mr 11:23-24).*

10. Expect deliverance and healing to manifest in your body and anticipate your situation to change. Expect the Lord to perform His Word in your life and affairs by **continually saying** *"Lord, you are now working in my body bringing about a cure and a healing".*

11. Fight the good fight of faith clothed in the full armor of God *(cf. Eph 6:10-18; 1 Ti 6:12)*.

12. Give God praise and glory for His goodness to you. Be a thankful believer, filled with gratitude for God's goodness.

■ ■ ■

The knowledge of the truth he acted upon had made him free and God will make and keep us free too.

When we are filled with the knowledge of God's will it enables us to be fortified and equipped to deal with the problems of life. Paul gives us an anointed prayer in *Ephesians 1:17-19* that we should pray over our lives daily:

> *That the God of our Lord Jesus Christ, the Father of glory, may give unto you the spirit of wisdom and revelation in the knowledge of him: The eyes of your understanding being enlightened; that ye may know what is the hope of his calling, and what the riches of the glory of his inheritance in the saints, And what is the exceeding greatness of his power to us-ward who believe, according to the working of his mighty power.*

This book is an overview study on the *Book of Job*, and I trust it will help you gain a better understanding of the source of Job's problems and bring revelation on how Satan was able to do his evil work.

Don't Jeopardize Your Life

Search the Scriptures yourself. God wants us to learn and benefit from knowing how God brought revelation and understanding to Job, so that he could receive deliverance and restoration in his life, family, and business.

We know there have been some very difficult situations God's people have gone through, and many are presently dealing with seeming unbearable trouble. We by no means have all the answers, we only know what the Word of God says regarding good and evil.

God is good and the Devil is evil! God's goodness, mercy, and deliverance are available to those who believe.

I have the utmost empathy for those who are suffering sickness and disease and have suffered great loss in their lives. This ministry is committed to preach, teach, and declare the Gospel of the Lord Jesus Christ in the love of God without compromise.

Jesus went about doing good, healing all who were **oppressed of the devil**, for God was with Him *(cf. Ac 10:38)*. Jesus Himself commissioned His people to go into all the world and preach the gospel to every creature so that they might have the opportunity of receiving and believing the good news, and be made free from the law of sin and death and experience the law of the spirit of life in Christ Jesus *(cf. Ro 8: 2)*. His will is for you to step into an overcoming life of love, peace, joy, healing, wholeness and abundance *(cf. 3 Jo 2)*.

Do you feel you are like Job? Then do what Job did—he got himself out of his miserable situation by gaining correct knowledge of the ways and purposes of God.

Secondly, Job humbled himself and repented of his foolish talk and he prayed for his friends who had tried to comfort and instruct him out of their own lack of godly wisdom or compassion.

Then God did the miraculous! His physical and mental suffering came to an end. God turned his captivity and restored to him twice as much as he had in the beginning.

Let your captivity be turned today and enjoy the fullness of the blessings of your Heavenly Father.

The Gospel is good news! Freedom from sin is good news! Freedom from the curse is good news. Healing, health, and prosperity are good news! Knowing you can live a victorious and holy life because you have been made the righteousness of God in Christ is good news! *(cf. 2 Co 5:21)*

Live in the light of the knowledge of the goodness of God. Let Him bless you today and everyday!

Chapter 8

Revelation Truths that Agree with New Testament Benefits

We cannot forget to address the beautiful prophetic words that were inspired by the Holy Spirit through the writer of the *book of Job.*

We are not sure if Job fully understood the prophetic utterances given through the Holy Spirit. They are beautifully inserted throughout the book, which in turn is for our learning and edification.

These revelations are in complete agreement with the Word of God and New Testament realities.

I know My Redeemer Lives

For I know that my redeemer liveth, and that he shall stand at the latter day upon the earth. And though after my skin worms destroy this body, yet in my flesh shall I see God. - Job 19:26-27

This statement is of divine inspiration revealed to Job by the Revealer of Truth, the blessed Holy Spirit.

In Revelations we are told that every eye shall see Jesus when He comes in the clouds of glory.

Behold, he cometh with clouds; and every eye shall see him ..." - Revelation 1:7

And they shall see his face; and his name shall be in their foreheads. - Revelation 22:4

You Shall Declare a Thing and it Shall be Established

Thou shalt also decree a thing, and it shall be established unto thee: and the light shall shine upon thy ways. - Job 22:26

This is an amazing revelation given to Job. Knowing the time line of the writing of this book, there were no written revelations of the will and purpose of God for mankind. Job actually spoke in line with *Mark 11:23 and 24* the words of Jesus, concerning how the God kind of faith works.

Years later Solomon wrote these powerful words:

Life and death are in the power of the tongue: and they that love it shall eat the fruit thereof. - Proverbs 18:21

Jesus confirmed this in the New Testament.

For by thy words thou shalt be justified, and by thy words thou shalt be condemned. - Matthew 12:37

The Apostle Paul gives us another witness to this divine revelation regarding the power of our words.

...That thou mightest be justified in thy sayings, and mightest overcome when thou are judged. - Romans 3:4

I Have Found a Ransom

But if a special messenger from heaven is there to intercede for a person, to declare that he is upright, God will be gracious and say, Set him free. Do not make him die, for I have found a ransom for his life. Then his body will become as healthy as a child's, firm and youthful again. When he prays to God, he will be accepted. And God will receive him with joy and restore him to good standing. - Job 33:24-26 NLT

What a powerful and relevant revelation! Did Job fully understand what he uttered? Perhaps not, but we have a Bible that declares to us Who our Ransom and Redeemer is and what He did to pay for our complete redemption from sin, sickness, poverty and all the effects of the curse of the law.

Eliphaz, the Temanite uttered a wonderful word in *Job 5:26* concerning longevity.

Thou shalt come to thy grave in a full age, like as a shock of corn cometh in his season. - Job 5:26

If Only There Were a Mediator

If only there would be a mediator who could bring us together, but there is none. The mediator could make God stop beating me, and I would no longer live in terror of his punishment. Then I could speak to him without fear, but I cannot do that in my own strength. - Job 9:33-35 NLT

The deep heart cry of Job is expressed in these verses—He is crying out for one who could successfully mediate for him. One who would represent him in his time of agony and suffering at the hands of the Adversary, Satan himself. Unfortunately Job thought that God was punishing him through beating him.

Job knew of no one who could represent him as he stood in his excruciating trial. He felt all alone and completely forsaken. His cry was on behalf of all mankind who stands in the court of hopeless condemnation and judgment. In his ignorance Job thought God was responsible for beating him and causing such terror of punishment and fear. He knew he could do nothing in his own strength.

It was a plea for an intercessor, one who would stand in the gap and take his place of suffering and retribution. Thank

God, we have an intercessor and mediator Who stood in the courts of divine justice and pled our case, took our place, and made us completely free.

■ ■ ■

Let your captivity be turned today and enjoy the fullness of the blessings of your Heavenly Father.

Our New Testament reveals the One Who came and gave His life a ransom for all mankind, His Name is Jesus! He is the One and only mediator! God initiated the master plan to release us from the curse of the law.

For there is one God, and one mediator between God and men, the man Christ Jesus; Who gave himself a ransom for all, to be testified in due time.
- 1 Timothy 2:5-6

There is only one God and one Mediator who can reconcile God and humanity—the man Christ Jesus. He gave his life to purchase freedom for everyone. This is the message God gave to the world at just the right time. - 1 Timothy 2: 5-6 NLT

Divine Prosperity

If thou return to the Almighty, thou shalt be built up, thou shalt put away iniquity far from thy tabernacles.

Then shalt thou lay up gold as dust, and the gold of Ophir as the stones of the brooks. Yea, the Almighty shall be thy defence (gold) and thou shalt have plenty of silver. - Job 22:23 - 25

These words inspired by the Holy Spirit through Eliphaz once again reveals to us that God's plan of redemption includes financial and material prosperity. The curse of poverty must be atoned for along with sin and sickness.

Job had been the richest man in the east at the time this book was written *(cf. Job 1:3)*. Satan came and stole it from him through Job's ignorance of Satan's devices and schemes. However, we can read of Job's end and how God restored to him double of all that had been stolen from him *(cf. Job 42:10)*.

The young man Elihu further writes with accuracy, revealing to us the will of God concerning financial prosperity in the following verses:

If they obey and serve him, they shall spend their days in prosperity, and their years in pleasures. But if they obey not they shall perish by the sword, and they shall die without knowledge. - Job 36:11-12

This proves how vital it is for believers to study the Scriptures and allow the Holy Spirit to reveal to them the will and purpose of God. Without an accurate knowledge of

Revelation Truths that Agree with...

the Word of God the enemy can so easily steal, kill, and destroy *(cf. Joh 10:10)*.

Study to show thyself approved unto God, a workman that needeth not to be ashamed, rightly dividing the word of truth. - 2 Timothy 2:15

All Scripture is given by inspiration of God, and is profitable for doctrine, for reproof, for correction, for instruction in righteousness: That the man of God may be perfect, throughly furnished unto all good works. - 2 Timothy 3:16-17

JOB'S JEOPARDY

Chapter 9

Chastisement: Correction or Punishment

W hat does the word *chastisement* mean to you? What picture or image does it convey to your understanding? It will mean different things to different people.

In a religious setting it could give one a mental picture of God holding a whip ready to inflict horrible punishment and pain on His disobedient children. But we want to know what the word *chastisement* means according to the Word of God.

First and foremost we must understand that God is a very good Father God to His children, those born again of His Spirit and the Word of God. The riches of His goodness and forbearance and longsuffering have a divine purpose and that is to lead the lost to repentance (cf. Ro 2:4). God's ways are far higher than our ways, His thoughts far higher than our thoughts *(cf. Isa 55:8-9)*. That does not mean we cannot know His ways or purposes. In fact, it is imperative that we understand His dealings with the world and His children. He operates on a far higher level than any earthly parent and He not only desires the very best for us but He has provided for us that we might enjoy His surpassing goodness.

And ye have forgotten the exhortation which speaketh unto you as unto children, My son, despise not thou the chastening of the Lord, nor faint when thou art rebuked of him:
For whom the Lord loveth he chasteneth, and scourgeth every son whom he receiveth.
If ye endure chastening, God dealeth with you as with sons; for what son is he whom the father chasteneth not?
But if he be without chastisement, whereof all are partakers, then are ye bastards (illegitimate offspring), and not sons.
Furthermore, we have had fathers of our flesh which corrected us, and we gave them reverence: shall we not much rather be in subjection to the Father of spirits, and live?
For they verily for a few days chastened us after their own pleasure; but he for our profit, that we might be partakers of his holiness.
Now no chastening for the present seemeth to be joyous, but grievous: nevertheless afterward it yieldeth the peaceable fruit of righteousness unto them which are exercised thereby. - Hebrews 12:5-11

God, our Heavenly Father does chasten His children, otherwise we would be called "illegitimate" and we would not be one of His. The question is, How does God chasten us?

Chastisement: Correction or Punishment

What is His mode of operation? Does it mean broken legs, a broken marriage, accidents, calamities, sickness, or broken lives with pain and suffering?

It would be well to understand the meaning of the word *chasten* as used in the Scriptures.

First, the word *chasten* does not mean **punishment**. All chastening as used in the Bible is a word that implies educative discipline.

The Hebrew word *(yasar)* in the Old Testament means: *to instruct, to correct, to teach, to reprove.* This word is used only one time to mean: *to punish.*

In *2 Timothy 2:25*: the same Greek word used here is: *instructing.*

In *1 Timothy 1:20*: the same Greek word used here is: *to learn or learning.*

In *Acts 22:3*: the same Greek word used here is: *taught or teaching.*

The Purpose of Chastening

Chastening is for the building of godly character—God's character and nature within our spirit, thus affecting our mind and flesh, bringing it under divine discipline and changing our outward conduct. It is for our profit that we might be sharers of His holiness *(cf. Heb 12:10).*

■ ■ ■

He operates on a far higher level than any earthly parent and He not only desires the very best for us but He has provided for us that we might enjoy His surpassing goodness.

Children left by themselves, without parental training and instruction on how to live uprightly and obedient, with respect for others and themselves, become rebellious and not fit to live in society. Child training is ongoing, day by day, but it does reap a valuable harvest in the lives of those being instructed in the right way to live.

Undisciplined children are a sorrow and bring grief to their parents. They grow up lawless and rebellious.

Foolishness is bound in the heart of a child and the rod of correction will drive it from him. - Proverbs 22:15

How Did Our Parents Discipline Us?
(Or Should Have!)

Hebrews 12:9:... we have had fathers of our flesh which corrected us ...

Chastisement: Correction or Punishment

Firstly, earthy fathers would discipline or train us with words and warnings.

Secondly, they might have deprived us of special treats and privileges.

Thirdly, they should have followed the Word of God by spanking us if we did not heed their words and reproof and continued in rebellion.

How Does God Discipline—Chasten—Teach or Correct His Children?

Our Heavenly Father, who is called the Father of spirits in *Hebrews 12: 9*, chastens us in the "spirit", not in the flesh. We are a spirit and we possess a soul (mind, will, and emotions) and live in a physical body. God's Words are spirit and they are life and they deal directly with our spirit man, bringing reproof, correction, and instruction in righteousness.

> *Every Scripture is God-breathed (given by His inspiration) and profitable for instruction, for reproof and conviction of sin, for correction of error and discipline in obedience, [and] for training in righteousness (in holy living, in conformity to God's will in thought, purpose, and action), so that the man of God may be complete and proficient, well fitted and thoroughly equipped for every good work. - 2 Timothy 3:16-17 AMP*

The purpose of His Word is to bring correction so that *the man of God may be perfect, thoroughly furnished unto all good works.*

God, our Heavenly Father, does not chasten us with anything that would steal, kill or destroy us. Jesus plainly tells us who does the stealing, killing, and destroying *(cf. Joh 10:10).* That means He does not use physical things to chasten us, He deals with our spirit. He does not send sickness, disease, pain, or poverty, accidents or anything that would physically harm us. God has no sickness to give us. He is not confused, double-minded or a child abuser! Jesus said God is not divided against Himself, else His Kingdom will not stand *(cf. Mt 12:25).*

Keep in mind that the mentality of the people in the Old Testament was: *If God permits it He commits it.* Dr. Robert Young, a well respected theologian, points out the translation from the Hebrew, for example, the words *to smite* should have been translated *allow to be smitten.* Verbs like these were translated into English in the causative tense rather than the permissive tense, as it was originally written in Hebrew.

When a believer is sick it *could* be a result of personal sin *(cf. Jas 5:15)* but even then sin will be forgiven when the prayer of faith is offered. Then again the sickness may be none other than a direct attack of the enemy to steal his health. When one is sick do not pray and ask God to keep the sickness on you to teach you.

Remember, God's ways are higher than our ways. Paul says in *Romans 2:4* that *it is the goodness of God that leads to repentance.* Healing and prosperity and total well-being are the goodness of God manifested. God will allow anything we allow or permit in our lives, for He has given all of us freedom to choose—life or death.

If we permit sin and it is not repented of, then we reap the harvest. It is far better to discipline our flesh before sin is conceived and it brings forth a bad harvest. You see, God will continue to deal with a believer in sin and do everything He can to bring him to repentance. But why learn the hard way?

■ ■ ■

The purpose of His Word is to bring correction so that the man of God may be perfect, thoroughly furnished unto all good works.

First Corinthians 11:31-32 says that we can and should judge or chasten (examine) ourselves so that we are not judged. *But when we are judged, we are chastened of the Lord, that we should not be condemned with the world.* We will save ourselves weakness, sickness, and even premature death if we will heed these words of correction and instruction.

How Did God Chasten His Church
In The New Testament?

When we look at the seven churches in Asia Minor we see how God dealt with His people in these churches. *(cf. Re 2-3)*

1. Firstly, He commended them for their works—–what they were doing right.

2. Then He told them what they were doing wrong and what needed to be corrected.

3. Repent was the next word He commanded them to do. So God will tell you how to change the situation.

4. Then He told them to hear what the Spirit says to the churches.

God's Word brought correction and instruction in righteousness. The Holy Spirit is the teacher of the Church *(cf. Joh 14:26)*.

If a believer does not heed the corrective words of the Holy Spirit then the blessings are forfeited by putting oneself in the realm of the curse again.

Correction is not a joyous experience to the flesh or mind but it is profitable—it yields the peaceful fruit of righteousness to those who humbly allow themselves to be

Chastisement: Correction or Punishment

disciplined and trained by the Word and the Holy Spirit. *(cf. Heb 12)*

Allow God to chasten you the way He wants to through His Spirit and by the Word of God. Or else you will have to learn the hard way and Satan will really make it hard!

O give thanks unto the Lord, for He is good: for his mercy endures forever! - Psalms 107:1

About the Author

(Continued from back cover) ... She has also ministered for women's conferences in the United States and hosted Faith Women International conferences in Amsterdam, Brussels, London; Bermuda and other European cities. Barbara follows the call of God on her life from early childhood.

For over fifty years she and her husband Gordon traveled and ministered together on six continents. Their anointed husband and wife ministry began in the United Kingdom, followed by pastoral ministry in the United States. From 1988 they flowed in the prophets anointing to the nations. Throughout their pastoral and international ministry, the Lord was pleased to confirm His word through many signs and wonders. By the anointing of the Holy Spirit, miracles, healing gifts and prophetic utterances have followed the preaching and teaching of God's Word.

Barbara's loving husband, Gordon White, was promoted to heaven on June 26, 2014. She continues to follow God's plan for her life, teaching faith, healing, and motivating the body of Christ to live in victory. Her ministry flows in the anointing with manifestations of the gifts of the Holy Spirit.

Barbara believes and continually shares that The Gospel is GOOD NEWS! Freedom from sin is GOOD NEWS! Freedom from the curse is GOOD NEWS. Healing, health, and prosperity are GOOD NEWS! Knowing you can live a victorious and holy life because you have been made the righteousness of God in Christ is GOOD NEWS!

Live in the light of the knowledge of the goodness of God. Let Him bless you today and everyday!

Her book *"Navigating Through The Maze of Grief"*, is an anointed book which is helping many heal from the pain of loss and grief.

Other books available by the Author

- *Say The Word*
- *Our Love Journey:*
  Memoirs of Gordon & Barbara White's Ministry
- *Let Patience Work For You*

Barbara's Resources

Winning Widows is a group page on Facebook, devoted to ministering to the emotional support and spiritual needs of widows, and those who have lost loved ones. You are invited to join this page to receive daily inspirational Bible devotions.

Faith Ministries International: Barbara's ministry page is available on Facebook. When you join you will receive monthly teaching newsletters and ministry updates.

Barbara is available to speak to your church, group, or teaching seminar.

www.fmint.org

Enjoy these other great books from Bold Truth Publishing

Seemed Good to THE HOLY GHOST
by Daryl P Holloman

Effective Prison Ministries
by Wayne W. Sanders

TURN OFF THE STEW
by Judy Spencer

The Holy Spirit SPEAKS Expressly
by Elizabeth Pruitt Sloan

Matthew 4:4
Man shall not live by bread alone...
by Rick McKnight

VICTIM TO VICTOR (THE CHOICE IS YOURS)
by Rachel V. Jeffries

SPIRITUAL BIRTHING
Bringing God's Plans & Purposes and Manifestation
by Lynn Whitlock Jones

BECOMING PERFECT
Let The Perfector Perfect His Work In You
by Sally Stokes Weiesnbach

FIVE SMOOTH STONES
by Aaron Jones

Available at select bookstores and
www.BoldTruthPublishing.com

Why do we confess the Word of God?
Did Jesus confess the Word of God?

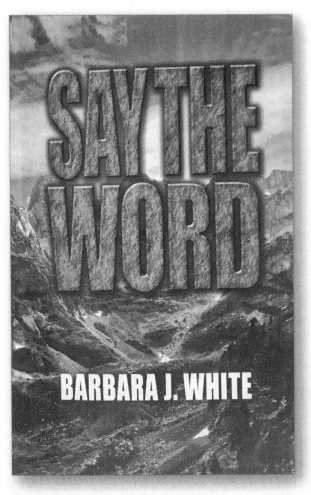

If you have been dismayed when trouble or crisis come your way, then *SAY THE WORD* will help you to understand the importance of saying what God says in His Word.

Available at select bookstores and
www.BoldTruthPublishing.com

In this book, the Author explores: what's on the other side of a death—for those of us still living?

- Surviving the loss of a loved one.
- Avoiding the grip of grief.
- Defeating loneliness and fear.
- How to face the future.

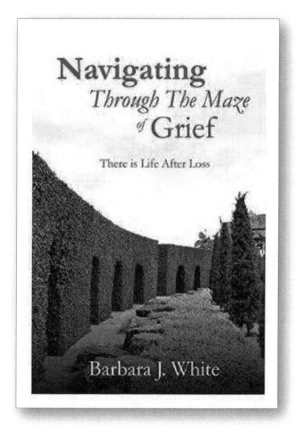

You are not alone as you walk through your maze of grief; there is a place called "the other side" waiting for you. It is a beautiful life of victory and joy.

Available at select bookstores and

www.BoldTruthPublishing.com

Made in the USA
San Bernardino, CA
14 November 2017